Color Friends™

Red
Yellow
Blue

Purple
Orange
Green

For my daughters, Lillian & Alexandria.
You bring the most beautiful colors to our world!

Library of Congress Control Number 2024902265
Published in the United States by Wild Child Education Co.
ISBN 978-1-7342645-5-5

For more information, to book an event or for other inquiries about this book
emails can be sent to the author at wildchildeducation@yahoo.com

This book belongs to:

____

____

These are the
color friends!
They are part of something called the
color wheel.

A color wheel shows us
the colors relationship to each other,
how the colors mix and how the colors
are created.

Primary Color - Red
Secondary Color - Purple
Secondary Color - Orange
Primary Color - Yellow
Primary Color - Blue
Secondary Color - Green

There are so many colors in the world around you, just look around!

There are three main colors that make them all!

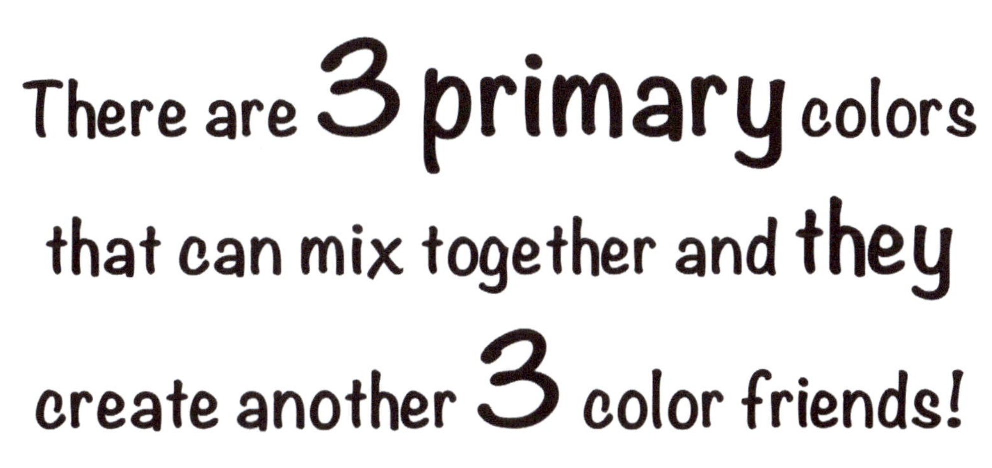

There are 3 primary colors that can mix together and they create another 3 color friends!

We call those the secondary colors.

Primary colors
can not be mixed from
other colors.
They are the source of
all other colors.

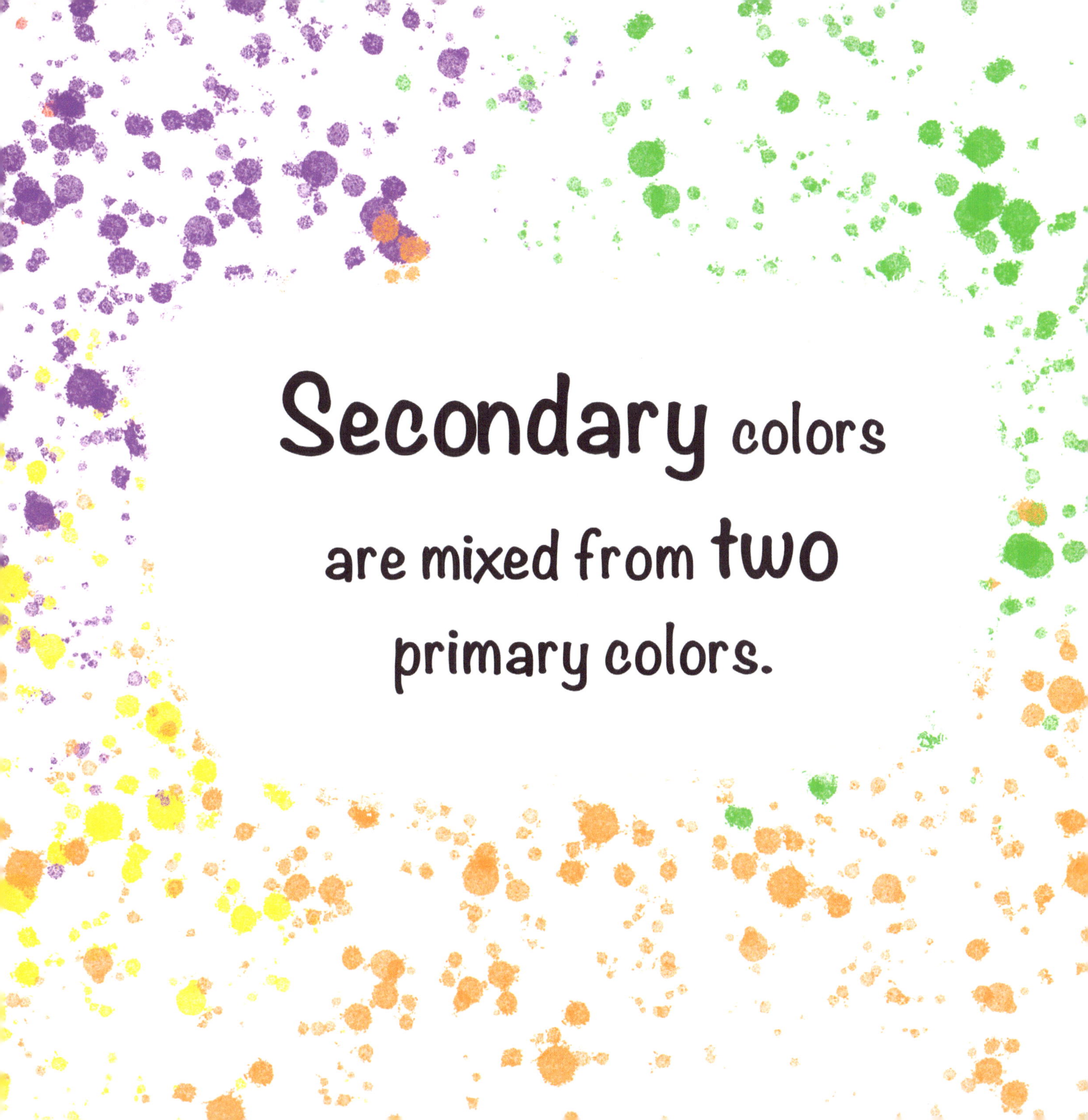

Secondary colors
are mixed from two
primary colors.

Red, Yellow and Blue

are primary colors!

Purple, Orange and Green

are **secondary**

colors!

Blue and Red were running too fast.
With their eyes closed, singing and enjoying
the feeling of movement when...

"Watch out!",
said a bird flying by.

As Blue and Red
bumped into each other, they fell to the ground.
Looking around, they noticed
another friend was there now.

It is Purple!

When you mix **Blue** and **Red**, it makes **Purple**!

Blue was playing in the pool.
Yellow saw this
and wanted to jump in, too!

"Aaaaaaaah!", said Blue.

As Yellow jumped in, Blue
noticed a new color in the pool.

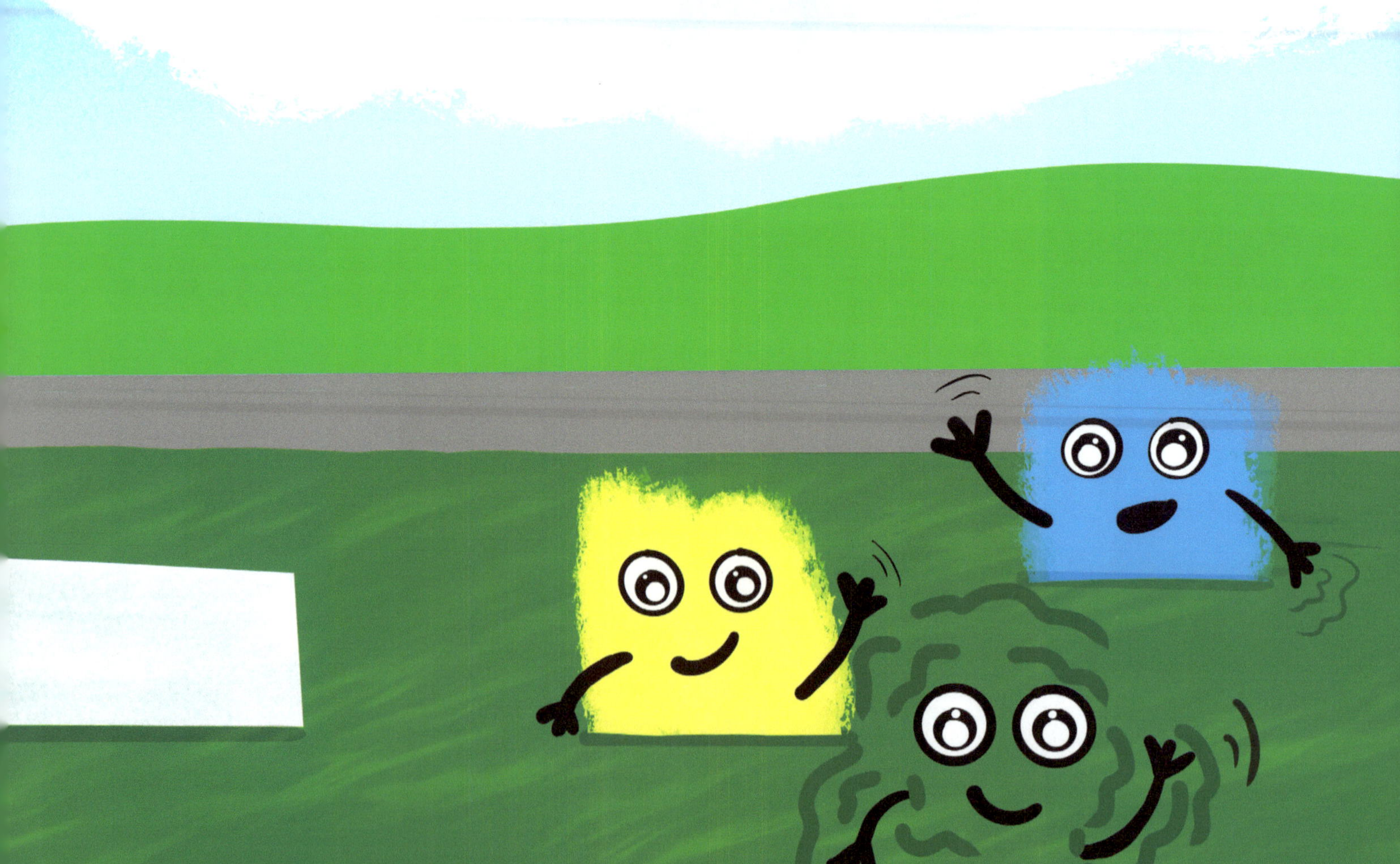

Green was in the water around them.

When you mix **Yellow** and **Blue**,
it makes **Green**!

Red and Yellow were
hard at work, creating their
own masterpieces.

When Yellow reached for
the paint bottle,

Ooops!

Yellow had tipped the paint bottles over.
"Sorry", said Yellow.

Red didn't get mad.
Red knew Yellow did it by accident
and they noticed something happened
when the two paints spilled together.

They made a new friend!

When you mix **Red** and **Yellow**, it makes **Orange**!

Can you remember the colors?

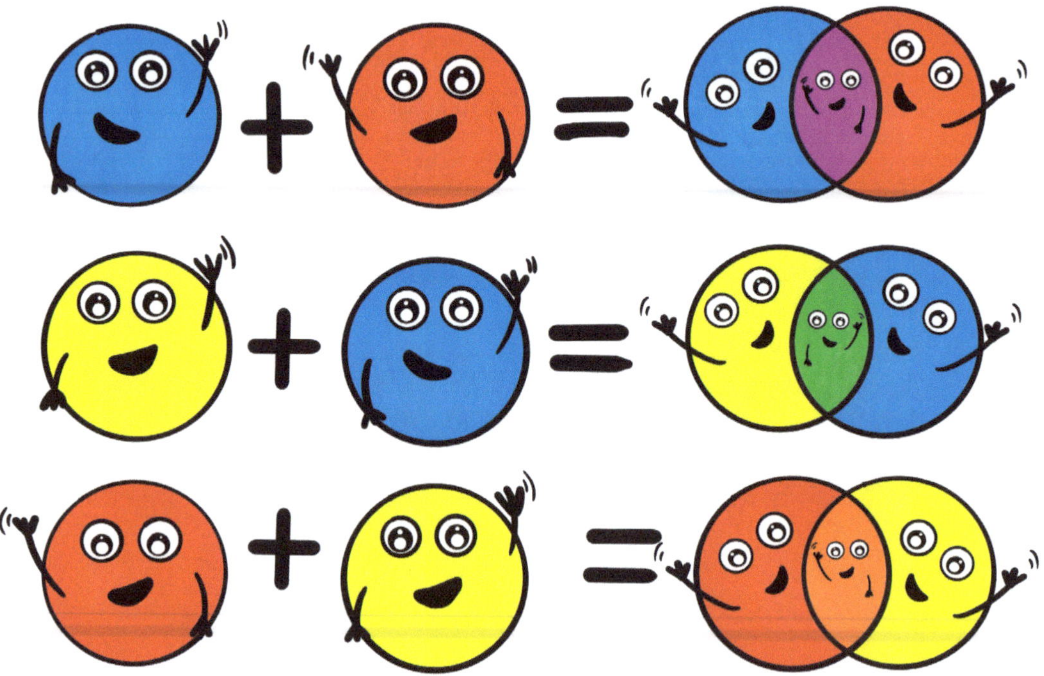

Point to and say each color.
Then say what color friend they make!

What will you make
and what colors
will you use?

Keep practicing!

Practice finding the colors by pointing them out in the things you see around you.
Practice at home, outside and anywhere you are!

Find and point out both primary and secondary colors!

Remember:

Primary color friends

Secondary color friends

Red
Yellow
Blue

Purple
Orange
Green